even more sermon illustrations

david adam

kevin mayhew

First published in 2008 by

KEVIN MAYHEW LTD
Buxhall, Stowmarket, Suffolk, IP14 3BW
E-mail: info@kevinmayhewltd.com
Web: www.kevinmayhew.com

Even More Sermon Illustrations is extracted from *Searchlights,* Complete Resource Book, Year A.

Acknowledgements:

Jesus is the way, page 34: And I said to the man . . . (Minnie Louise Haskins), taken from a collection called *Desert,* © Minnie Louise Haskins, 1908.

Good News in dark times, page 64: Though the dawn breaks cheerless . . . *Hebridean Altars,* (Alistair MacLean), Hodder & Stoughton, 1937.

9 8 7 6 5 4 3 2 1 0

ISBN 978 1 84417 877 3
Catalogue No 1501058

Cover design by Sara-Jane Came
Edited by Katherine Laidler
Typesetting by Richard Weaver

Printed in Great Britain

Contents

Introduction

This third book of sermon illustrations was compiled with the busy minister, preacher or speaker in mind: it can be a daunting task to find a fresh theme or topic each week and these short pieces will hopefully be a handy resource. They are meant to help provide that sometimes elusive topic or to amplify an existing central theme.

Visual aids often speak more directly than words and these short, vivid illustrations, as well as illustrations from your locality, can help you to throw light on the Scripture passages and to relate them to what is happening in your community or the world.

By referring to the two indexes (Topical and Bible reference) you can decide how to plan the sermon or expand on your own theme. The cross-referencing means that you have quite a few ideas at your fingertips.

1 Never put off today . . .

Aim

To be awake to Christ's coming to us today.

Reading

Matthew 24:36-44

Illustration

When the devil wanted to ruin the lives of many people he called a meeting of his fallen angels and sought suggestions. 'I will tell them there is no God,' said the first. The devil replied, 'Any sensitive and thinking person knows there is a God and this will not lead them astray.' A second said, 'I will tell them there is no hell.'

'What is the use of that?' asked the evil one. 'Everyone will experience a taste of hell and know that it is a reality.'

A third then spoke up and said, 'I will tell them there is no hurry. Put it off until tomorrow – for I know tomorrow never comes.' With this the devil was delighted and this is how most people fail to turn to God.

Pablo Picasso said, 'Never put off today anything that you do not want to leave undone for ever.'

2 Be prepared

Aim

To prepare for the coming of the Lord.

Reading

Matthew 3:1-12

Illustration

Making a journey was not easy in biblical times. An eastern proverb goes, 'There are three states of misery: illness, fasting and travel.' Before anyone went on a journey they were advised to 'pay all debts, provide for dependants, provide parting gifts, return all articles under trust, take money and a good temper, then bid farewell to all'. Roads were often in poor condition, full of holes and bumps that made travel difficult if not dangerous. Journeying was never done for pleasure. There were few cared-for roads. Josephus tells us that King Solomon laid a causeway of black basalt stone along the roads that led to Jerusalem 'to manifest the grandeur of his riches and government'. All surfaces and built-up roads were originally built for the king and for his use. Before the king was due to visit an area, the inhabitants were visited and warned to be ready. They had to make sure the road didn't have any obstacles to make the king's journey difficult. They also had to be prepared to welcome him. John the Baptist is to be seen as one who tells us of the need to prepare the way for the coming of the King, of the Christ.

3 Practise what you preach

Aim

To show that actions speak louder than words.

Reading

Matthew 11:2-11

Illustration

When Bede writes about St Aidan he says, 'The highest recommendation of his teaching to all was that he and his followers lived as they taught. He never sought or cared for any worldly possession, and loved to give away to the poor who chanced to meet him whatever he received from kings or wealthy folk. Whether in town or country, he always travelled on foot unless compelled by necessity to ride; and whoever the people he met on his walks, whether high or low, he stopped and spoke to them. If they were heathen, he urged them to be baptised; and if they were Christians, he strengthened their faith and inspired them by word and deed to live a good life and to be generous to others.'

It was the example of a life lived for God that spoke out louder than the words he spoke and backed up what he preached.

4 Perfect freedom

Aim

To show that true freedom comes from loving and serving God.

Reading

Romans 8:18-30

Illustration

Ivan lived under an oppressive regime. If those in power wanted anything, they took it. If they wanted you to do something, you had to do it or your life was at risk. The state police did not knock on doors; they forced their way into people's homes, and if they wanted anything, they took it. Everyone lived in fear and was oppressed. It was during this time that Ivan learnt the Good News of the Gospel. God did not force himself on people. He waited for Mary and Joseph to agree to his plans. In Jesus he did not oppress people but liberated them. Jesus did not burst into lives but said, 'I stand at the door and knock.' Ivan was amazed that so many ignored this loving, saving God. From the moment Ivan heard of such a God he sought to serve in that service which is 'perfect freedom'.

5 Make room for Jesus

Aim

To understand that we need to make room for Jesus in our lives.

Reading

John 1:1-14

Illustration

Nan-in was a great Japanese teacher of the art of Zen. One day a university professor came to seek some teaching. Nan-in served the traditional tea to his guest. He poured until his visitor's bowl was full and then kept pouring and the tea overflowed, as there was no room for it in the bowl. The professor watched until he could no longer restrain himself and said, 'It is overfull and no more will go in.' Nan-in said, 'You are like this cup. You are full of ideas and speculations. How can I pour more in unless you empty your cup? You need to make space to learn.'

In the same way we need to make a space in our lives each day for our God who comes to us.

Think upon these words by Angelus Silesius:

Though Christ a thousand times
in Bethlehem be born,
if he is not born in you,
you are still forlorn.

6 God who protects us

Aim

To show that God protects us in times of danger.

Reading

Matthew 2:13-23

Illustration

There are many stories of how people have been protected by angels; this one is from Vanuatu (the New Hebrides). The Reverend John Paton went as a missionary to the Hebridean Islands. One night a group of hostile natives surrounded his mission and home. Paton prayed for God to protect him. When morning came Paton was amazed to see his attackers leaving. About a year later the chief accepted Christianity and became a believer. The Reverend John asked him why they had not attacked his house and burned it down. The chief in turn asked him, 'Who were those men you had with you there?'

John replied, 'There were no men, only my wife and I.' The chief argued that he saw many men, big men in shining white garments with drawn swords standing guard.

7 Heaven here and now

Aim

To rejoice that heaven is not some far-off place but somewhere we should be living in now.

Reading

John 1:(1-9), 10-18

Illustration

A woman from County Kerry in Ireland was asked, 'Where is heaven?' She thought for a moment and then replied, 'About one foot and six inches above me.' She wanted to show that God and heaven are always close at hand and not beyond our reach. We have to just stretch ourselves, extend our vision, give the kingdom of heaven some priority in our life to begin to realise we are there. By giving time and attention to God we learn that 'we dwell in him and he in us'.

8 Many roads to God

Aim

To take encouragement from the example of the wise men in our own journey of faith.

Reading

Matthew 2:1-12

Illustration

There are many roads to God. God calls each of us and waits for our response. In the wise men we see at least three different roads. Perhaps they travelled alone and on different paths at the outset. Their faith journey brought them together.

Gold is a symbol of all God's gifts. All things come from God and of his own do we offer. God gives us life and this wonderful world. Many come to God through thanksgiving, through gratitude for all that he gives. Gold is also a symbol of power: wealth helps people to achieve and poverty restricts people.

Frankincense is symbol of awe, of mystery and adoration. If we are sensitive to the wonders of the world and the mystery of creation, this can lead us to God. This in turn can lead us to respect all of creation because it is of God. Frankincense is used in worship and many people learn of God through the worship of others.

Myrrh is a symbol of pain and the need for relief from pain and sorrow. For many it is easy to forget God in the good times. But when we lose a loved one or become seriously ill ourselves, it makes us ask questions about our existence. As mortals we all need the salvation and healing that God gives.

9 Love one another

Aim

To show that Jesus makes all the difference.

Readings

Matthew 3:13-17
1 John 4:7-21

Illustration

What a difference Jesus makes. *The Miracle of the River Kwai* by Ernest Gordon tells the story of prisoners of war building a bridge. They were overworked, often starving, exhausted and ill. The need to survive made them put themselves first and fail to see each other's needs. Then two men, Dusty and Dinty, began helping others. They put themselves out to care for and respect others. A new spirit began to spread through the camp until the place was transformed, as were its inhabitants. When questioned about their actions, Dusty read from 1 John 4:21: 'The commandment we have from him is this: those who love God must love their brothers and sisters also.' Dusty was a Methodist and Dinty a Roman Catholic, and both were full of the Presence. The lives of the men had been hell. Then 'Jesus came' and what a difference that made.

10 Bringing others to Jesus

Aim

To show the importance of bringing people to Jesus.

Reading

John 1:29-42

Illustration

It is often proclaimed that the Church is suffering from a crisis in the West. There is a shortage of priests, of ministers. Allied to this is a shortage of money. But more money or more clergy will not cure the crisis. The Church needs a dose of Andrews! It needs people who will abide with Christ and then bring others to Christ. The Church is not short of people and it could grow as it did of old if we would learn to abide with Christ and seek to bring others to him.

The Church grew from twelve disciples who were with Jesus and who wanted others to know him. We must learn to bring others to the One we know and love. Just think how quickly the Church would grow if we were all committed to bringing someone else to know Jesus.

11 Giving ourselves to God

Aim
To encourage people to respond to the call of God.

Reading
Matthew 4:12-23

Illustration
There are two stories of Socrates and his calling of disciples. Xenophon met Socrates on the road and the teacher barred his path with a stick. Socrates asked Xenophon simple questions about where certain things were made. Then he asked, 'Do you know where men are made good and virtuous?'

'No, I do not,' answered the young man. Socrates then said, 'Follow me and learn.'

On another occasion a man called Aeschines came to Socrates and said, 'I am a poor man, I have nothing else to offer but myself.' Socrates replied, 'Do you not see that you are giving me the most precious thing of all?'

It is in giving ourselves to God that we truly give.

12 God's transforming power

Aim

To show God meets our lack of resources with his abundant power and generosity.

Reading

John 2:1-11

Illustration

Charles was a relatively new Christian. He had a good home, a job and a loving family. Not long before it had been all endangered through Charles drinking too often. He said he could not help it. Whenever his resources were low, whenever he felt tired or exhausted, he turned to the bottle. His family were suffering; they did not have enough income to survive on after Charles's drinking. A friend introduced him to Alcoholics Anonymous and also to his local church. The second had an amazing effect. Charles discovered the power of the love and presence of God. Now when resources were low or when he felt exhausted, he turned to rest in God and to be renewed by him. At a Bible study he expressed difficulty with the miracle of changing water into wine. 'But,' he said, 'I know Jesus can change lives. He can turn wine into food on the table and to clothes on our backs.' Jesus has the power to renew and refresh each of us in our lives.

13 The light of Christ

Aim

To let the light of Christ enter our hearts and our lives.

Reading

Luke 2:22-40

Illustration

The night was pitch black as the car drove along a country lane. There were no lights for miles. Suddenly the driver was aware that a rear tyre had a puncture. He would have to stop and mend it. Once out of the car he could see very little. The lights of the car did not give light where he wanted it and he had no torch. This would be a very slow job and he was not sure he could do it in the dark. It was worrying because he was a long way from any houses and it was very late at night. Fortunately, within a few minutes he saw a light coming along the road in front of him. It was a milkman on his early rounds. Though he was busy, the milkman stopped and provided light and what a difference that made. The man no longer worked in darkness but in the light.

14 The light of the world

Aim

To look at what it means to be the light of the world.

Reading

Matthew 5:14-20

Illustration

A man bought a special gift for his wife. It was a musical box that played a tune when you opened it, but it was different because it also glowed in the dark. It was meant to be seen when the days were dark or dull. As it was a present, he kept the box hidden away and all wrapped up. At last he produced it one dark evening and his wife unwrapped it with great excitement. They turned the lights off, but then it could not be seen. It did not glow in the dark, and they were disappointed. Perhaps it was broken. They put the lights back on and discovered a label inside the box that said, 'If you want me to shine all night, keep me in the sun all day.'

There was nothing wrong with the box, and once they left it in the sunlight, it glowed in the dark.

In the same way if we are to be lights in the world, we must spend time each day absorbing the light of Christ.

15 Made in his image

Aim

To show how our lives should reflect the love of God because we are made in his image.

Reading

Matthew 5:43-48

Illustration

One of the Great Masters was painting the Last Supper. The painting was coming along well until he had a violent row with a friend. He went home full of anger and painted on to the canvas his friend as Judas. This would serve to remind him of the row between them; it would keep his anger warm. Now there was little of the painting to finish, only the central character which was the Christ. But the vision would not come. Hand and eye did not work as they should and the canvas was left unfinished. The hatred of the Judas figure was destroying peace of mind and preventing creative work. The anger in the mind left no room for vision. After weeks the canvas was untouched. He met his former friend and now felt ashamed of what he had done. He expressed sorrow to his friend and they were reunited. The artist went home and changed Judas and then painted his friend in the Christ place. The friendship had been restored and so the canvas completed.

16 Trust in God

Aim

To encourage a deeper trust in God and to stop worrying.

Reading

Matthew 6:25-34

Illustration

Imagine two people going for a walk together. Both have a difficult task to perform later in the day: a task that will take all their energy and ability.

One man cannot get it out of his mind. He turns it over and over. He does not notice the sunshine or the birds singing. He fails to notice the beauty that is all around him. He may as well be indoors and working.

The other man relaxes for a while in the sunshine. He enjoys the heat of the sun and the sound of the birds. He is aware of the good things around him. He watches a butterfly with delight. This man is being refreshed and restored, ready for the work ahead.

One carried his worries and they wore him down. The other took time off and was refreshed for the job ahead. It is too easy to let worry and anxiety prevent us from enjoying the present moment and steal any energy we have.

17 God's glory revealed

Aim

To show that God reveals his glory in his Son Jesus Christ.

Reading

Matthew 17:1-9

Illustration

As dark clouds cover the sun, so it is easy to let the dark events of life hide from us the glory and the presence of our God. It is then we need know that, even when we lose our grip, we are in the hand of God and in the heart of his Son who says to us, 'Arise, do not be afraid.'

You might like to affirm the words written by a Jewish prisoner on a wall in Cologne:

> I believe in the sun even when it is not shining.
> I believe in love even when I cannot feel it.
> I believe in God even when he is silent.

18 Temptation

Aim

To show that temptation is the norm if we are truly alive.

Reading

Matthew 4:1-11

Illustration

One of the Desert Fathers prayed that all his passions should be taken away so that he would not be tempted. He then went to one of the Elders and said, 'You see before you a man who is not tempted and is at rest.' The Elder replied, 'Go and pray that some struggle is stirred up in you for the soul only matures through its battles against evil.' The monk did as he was asked and when temptation came he didn't ask to escape it but instead prayed, 'Lord, give me strength to get through the fight.'

Temptation is part of being alive to what is around us. We will be tempted as long as we live.

19 Jesus, our light and life

Aim

To show that through Jesus we can be reborn.

Reading

John 3:1-17

Illustration

There are many very clever and capable people (they are often also well-off) who feel they are missing out on something of the fullness of life. Listen to the words of Federico Fellini, the Italian film producer: 'Like so many people I have no religion and I just go sitting in a small boat drifting with the tide. I just go on working, cutting, shooting, editing and looking at life and trying to make others see. Today we stand naked and defenceless, more alone than at any time in history. We are waiting for something – perhaps another miracle, perhaps the Martians, who knows?'

Fellini, like Nicodemus, is in the dark, seeking someone or something that will deliver him from the darkness, from nothingness and death. A deliverer, a Saviour, is needed.

20 Jesus fills our emptiness

Aim

To show how Jesus fills our emptiness and our longing for God.

Reading

John 4:5-42

Illustration

Bill had tried everything to fill the gnawing emptiness that he felt inside. Whenever there was a time of quiet, the feeling of emptiness and worthlessness came upon him. He sought to escape into never having silence. Music, videos, computer games filled up his emptiness – but he knew it was still there. He tried to escape in thrills, in excitement, in sex and drugs. But underneath, the gnawing feeling was there. He felt alone and empty. One day, listening to the radio, Bill heard a poem by Francis Thompson called 'The Hound of Heaven'. The whole poem seemed to be about him. Certain lines, he said, struck home, especially these:

> 'All things betray thee, who betrayest me.'

> 'Naught shelters thee, who will not shelter me.'

And later:

> 'Lo! Naught contents thee, who content'st not me.'

He realised his emptiness was because he had been on the run from God. In tears, this big strong man committed himself to God in prayer. He started going to church and became a much more fulfilled and contented person. He came to love the Psalms and in particular Psalms 42 and 43.

21 A mother's love

Aim

To give thanks for all who love us, especially our mothers.

Readings

Luke 2:33-35
John 19:25b-27

Illustration

In J. K. Rowling's story of *Harry Potter and the Philosopher's Stone*, Quirrell, who is working for the wicked Voldemort, tries to kill Harry but is unable to do so even when he uses all the evil powers available to him. Harry asks Professor Dumbledore why Quirrell couldn't touch him and Dumbledore replies that Harry's mother died to save him, and if there was one thing Voldemort couldn't understand it was love. Love as powerful as hers for Harry left its own mark. Not a visible sign . . . but to have been loved so deeply, even though the person who loved us is gone, will give us some protection for ever.

22 The resurrection and the life

Aim

To show Jesus as the resurrection and the life.

Reading

John 11:1-45

Illustration

An American army chaplain tells how the raising of Lazarus affected one marine. There was a Bible study group on board a troopship returning from Japan. After studying this passage, a marine said, 'Everything is pointing at me.' The marine described how he had led a wild life and got into bad trouble. No one knew, except God. He felt guilty. He said his life was ruined and he could not face his family. He felt he was a dead man. 'But after reading this chapter, I have come alive again. I know that this resurrection Jesus was talking about is in the here and now, for he has raised me from death to life.' No doubt this man's troubles were not over, but in meeting Jesus he experienced the resurrection and the life.

23 The Prince of Peace

Aim

To know Jesus as the Prince of Peace.

Readings

Matthew 21:1-11
Psalm 118:1, 2, 19-29

Illustration

In a time when in some areas even the wearing of a cross is forbidden, and when the media are often pro-other faiths and anti-Christian, one Anglican bishop made a telling comment. He was asked why the Christians did not threaten with bombings and reprisals as some did. The bishop replied simply, 'We are not allowed to react like that: we follow the Prince of Peace.'

24 The living Lord

Aim

To enter into the wonder and joy of the resurrection.

Reading

John 20:1-18

Illustration

1066 is a date we all know: the Battle of Hastings. Did you know the Normans nearly lost the battle?

The English were behind a stockade. The Normans twice tried to break through. The second time they were repelled, it was rumoured that their leader was dead. The troops immediately began to lose heart. Soon they would be in headlong flight. William pulled off his helmet and rode among his troops shouting, 'I am alive. I am still alive.' The result was immediate: new courage, new strength of heart and purpose. This time they burst through the stockade and victory was won.

How like the state of the disciples after Good Friday. They had seen Jesus die; they had lost heart. And then, on that Easter morning, Jesus said to Mary, 'Tell them I am still alive.' What a difference his appearing would make to them and to the world.

25 The breath of life

Aim

To celebrate the hope that the resurrection brings.

Reading

John 20:19-21

Illustration

As a result of an explosion a small group of miners were trapped underground in a confined area. The phone to the surface still worked and they indicated they were all alive but they feared there was not enough air. It was realised that they would die without help – instant help. There was not much hope of getting them out alive. There were tons of earth to be removed and it was calculated it would be too late by the time it was done. With a special drill the rescue team bored a hole to where the men were and then pumped air into the cavern. Though it took another three days to get to them out, the men were found to be well and in good spirits. When one of them was asked what it was like he replied. 'A bit like the resurrection. We were sealed in a tomb unable to get out. Then we were given new air, the breath of life from the air pumped in to us. And then we were rescued and raised into the light.'

26 Meeting the risen Lord

Aim

To show that we meet Jesus the risen Lord in various ways.

Reading

Luke 24:13-35

Illustration

The Church in the Outer Hebrides rejoiced in the living Lord who could be met on the road and in the guise of a stranger. The following is an old poem from the Hebrides and now used by the Iona Community:

I saw a stranger at yestere'en.
I put food in the eating place,
drink in the drinking place,
music in the listening place,
and in the sacred name of the Triune
he blessed myself and my house,
my cattle and my dear ones,
and the lark said in her song,
'Often, often, often,
goes the Christ in the stranger's guise;
often, often, often,
goes the Christ in the stranger's guise.'

27 Jesus leads his flock

Aim

To know Jesus as the shepherd who leads us to life and life eternal.

Reading

John 10:1-10

Illustration

There is an old Jewish legend about why God chose Moses to be a leader of his people. When Moses was in the wilderness and caring for the sheep of his father-in-law, Jethro, a young lamb strayed away and got lost. Moses searched for it until he came to a deep dark ravine where it had gone down to find water. When Moses got to it he said, 'I did not know you ran away because you were thirsty. Now you must be very tired.' He took the lamb and put it on his shoulders and carried it back to safety. God said to Moses, 'Because you have cared for and brought back one of a flock belonging to man, you shall lead my flock Israel.'

28 Jesus is the way

Aim

To show that Jesus is with us on the journey of life and shows us the way.

Reading

John 14:1-14

Illustration

Often when we are feeling lost it is because we have wandered from him who is the way. More than any book of directions, we need to know God is with us on our journey.

> And I said to the man
> who stood at the gate of the year:
> Give me a light
> that I may tread safely into the unknown.
> And he replied:
> Go out into the darkness
> and put your hand in the Hand of God.
> That shall be to you better than a light
> and safer than a known way.

(From *Desert* by Minnie Louise Haskins, 1908, and quoted by King George VI in his Christmas broadcast, 25 December 1939.)

29 Love expressed in action

Aim

To show that loving God demands a response.

Reading

John 14:15-21

Illustration

How often do we fail to realise the cost of love in our homes? How our parents spend much of their lives giving themselves and what they have to us? Many of the household chores that are done for us are done not out of compulsion but out of love. But we should never take this for granted and the only way to respond to such love is to love in return. This, of course, would mean taking our share in the household tasks! Love is expressed in action. We do not do it because we have to – or because it is a rule of the house; we do it out of love for each other. True devotion is taking on some of the routine of caring for our home. Our failure in this work shows a lack of sensitivity and personal response to love.

30 At all times and in all places

Aim

To affirm that the presence of the ascended Lord is always with us.

Reading

Luke 24:44-53

Illustration

If the disciples were asked after the ascension, 'Where is Jesus now?' their reply would be very like the one that Longinus made to the wife of Pilate in John Masefield's *The Trial of Jesus*. Procula asks, 'Do you think he is dead?' To which Longinus replies, 'No, lady, I don't.' When asked, 'Then where is he?' Longinus replies, 'Let loose in all the world, lady.'

In the ascension we come to know that the Jesus who was limited by time and space is now able to be with all peoples at all times and in all places.

31 God with us

Aim

To show that eternal life comes from abiding in God and knowing he abides in us.

Reading

John 17:(1-11), 20-26

Illustration

In his diary for 1922 Shackleton writes of his Antarctic expedition:

> When I look back on those days, with all their anxiety and peril, I cannot doubt that our party was divinely guided both over snowfield and across storm-swept sea . . . I know that during that long racking march of thirty-six hours over unnamed mountains and glaciers of Southern Georgia it seemed to me we were not three but four. I said nothing to my companions on the point but afterwards Worsley said to me, 'Boss, I had a curious feeling in the march that there was another person with us.'

Do we affirm in our lives that our Lord is with us and travels with us wherever we go?

32 Filled with the Spirit

Aim

To proclaim and enjoy the fact that 'his Spirit is with us'.

Reading

Acts 2:1-21

Illustration

For a long time the flute seemed to lie around the house. It was not played and it gathered dust. Occasionally, someone would get it out and struggle to play a tune. It was decided that is was not a good instrument, perhaps useless and should be got rid of. This was mentioned to a friend of the family when he came to dinner. He asked that he might be able to handle it and play it. Mother had to dust it down before she gave it to him. Somehow it looked special as soon as it was in his hands. Once he started to play, the family were amazed at the beautiful sounds and music. This was a wonderful instrument and responded beautifully in the master's hands. It was just waiting for the touch of the master.

In many ways the disciples were like this until they were filled with the Spirit.

33 Father, Son and Holy Spirit

Aim

To encourage everyone to be Trinitarian in their faith and their prayers.

Reading

Matthew 28:16-20

Illustration

In the Hebrides, the islands off the west coast of Scotland, it was often difficult for a priest to get to some of the communities to baptise a new-born child. It became the tradition for the midwife to do a form of baptism that was known as the 'birth baptism'; later the child would be baptised in church and this was known as the 'great baptism' or the 'church baptism'. One such midwife said, 'When the image of the God of life is born into the world I put three little drops of water on the child's forehead. I put the first little drop in the name of the Father, and the watching-women say, "Amen." I put the second little drop in the name of the Son, and the watching-women say, "Amen." I put the third little drop in the name of the Spirit, and the watching-women say, "Amen." . . . All the people in the house are raising their voices, with the watching-women giving witness that the child has been committed to the blessed Trinity.'

Here is part of such a baptism prayer:

In the name of God,
in the name of Jesus,
in the name of the Spirit,
the perfect Three of power.

The little drop of the Father
on thy little forehead, beloved one.

The little drop of the Son
on thy little forehead, beloved one.

The little drop of the Spirit
on thy little forehead, beloved one.

To aid thee, to guard thee,
to shield thee, to surround thee.

34 Firm foundations

Aim

To encourage the building of a relationship with our God.

Reading

Matthew 7:21-29

Illustration

In the last century the cathedral at Winchester had restoration troubles. Great cracks were appearing in the structure. Experts suggested building buttresses to hold the cathedral up; others suggested great metal tie-bars to be placed across the cathedral to stop its walls falling outwards. One man insisted that they were only dealing with the symptoms of the trouble and the real cause was much deeper: he wanted to look at the foundations. He sunk a shaft into the ground and looked. He discovered the cathedral was built on a peat bog. The builders had laid tree trunks over the watery land and the cathedral was built on these. Due to improved drainage in the city the peat had dried out and shrunk. In many places there was a space between the cathedral and the ground below it. A man was employed for five and a half years to work underground in the removing of peat and putting in its place concrete blocks. Even a cathedral is only as firm as its foundations.

35 Transformed by his power

Aim

To look at the transforming power and love of Jesus.

Reading

Matthew 9:9-13, 18-26

Illustration

Jim had all the money he needed. It seemed whatever he did turned to gold. He had a great home and a lot of friends. He was able to spend a good deal of time enjoying himself. But Jim had an emptiness that nothing could fill. The more he tried to fill it with action, things or parties, the more it gnawed at him. He told a friend and the friend introduced him to a poem called 'The Hound of Heaven' by Francis Thompson. The line that worried the rich man was 'All things betray thee, who betrayest me'. The friend had the sense to tell him that he need not worry, for the hunger that he felt was none other than the calling of God in his life. 'Listen to God, respond to God and you will soon feel different.' Jim did as advised, he did not change his way of life or his friends, but he turned to God each day, started to worship each Sunday at his local church. He did not change but God changed him and he was now a far richer man than he had ever been.

36 Go out in my name

Aim

To show that those whom Jesus calls he also sends out.

Reading

Matthew 9:35–10:8-23

Illustration

Picture yourself coming to your own community and all the lights are out. The only light is coming from the church. You go to see where the light is coming from. It is coming from near the altar, so you approach the light. You see it is coming from a man sitting in a chair. You are about to ask him what he is doing and you see it is the Christ. You kneel before him. He does not move because he is a captive. He is tied to the chair, a prisoner. You ask him, 'Why are you tied, what has fixed you here?'

He replies, 'I am stuck here because my people will not reach out in love. My people do not proclaim the Good News. My people do not help in the healing of the nations. They have fastened me in the building.'

'Lord, how can I set you free?'

'By going out in my name and working with me in all the world.'

You offer yourself to his service, saying, 'Here I am, send me.' At that moment the Christ is freed and the lights begin to come on again.

37 God cares for us

Aim

To show how God cares for us, and how this should drive away fear.

Reading

Matthew 10:24-39

Illustration

Because Jesus says we need to fear God, he adds the balance of the fact that God values us and loves us. He talks of the sparrows in today's reading: 'Are not two sparrows sold for a penny? Yet not one of them falls to the ground without God noticing.' St Luke gives this in a slightly different form: 'Are not five sparrows sold for two pennies? Yet not one of them is forgotten in God's sight.' It would seem if the buyer was willing to buy four sparrows for two pence, a fifth was thrown in for free. It was as if the sparrow had no value at all! But God noticed and cared; God cares for all his creation.

When Jesus talks of one falling to the ground, it is easy to think of its death, and most people would not notice. But it may just mean land on the ground, to descend from flying. If God notices the small action of the sparrow, will he not all the more care for us?

38 Hospitality

Aim
To show how through hospitality Christ can be proclaimed and accepted.

Reading
Matthew 10:40-42

Illustration
The selfish giant banned the children from his garden. He built a wall around it and put up a notice saying:

TRESPASSERS
WILL BE
PROSECUTED

From that time spring did not come to the giant's garden and it remained winter. By keeping himself to himself, there was no warmth in the place.

Only when the children sneaked back did spring return with them. It was then that the giant realised his hostility to the children had kept him in the cold.

(Read the full story of the Selfish Giant in *The Happy Prince* by Oscar Wilde, Puffin Books.)

Hostility brings about isolation. Hospitality opens us to the warmth of relationships.

39 Responding to Jesus' call

Aim

To encourage people to respond to the welcoming call of Jesus and find rest.

Reading

Matthew 11:16-19, 25-30

Illustration

From *Pilgrim's Progress* by John Bunyan:

> He ran . . . till he came to the place somewhat ascending and on that place stood a cross . . . Just as Christian came up . . . his burden loosed from his shoulders and fell from off his back . . . I saw it no more.
>
> Then Christian glad and lightsome said with a merry heart, 'He has given me rest by his sorrow and life by his death' . . . it was very surprising to him that the cross should ease him of his burden . . . Then Christian gave three leaps for joy, and went on singing,
>
> > 'Thus far did I come laden with my sin
> > nor could ought ease the grief that was within
> > till I came hither: what place is this,
> > must be here the beginning of my bliss,
> > must here the burden fall from off my back,
> > must here the strings which bound it crack.
> > Blest Cross! Blest Sepulchre! Blest rather be
> > the man who was put to shame for me.'

40 Sowing seeds

Aim

To encourage more receptivity in our hearing and receiving of the Word.

Reading

Matthew 13:1-9, 18-23

Illustration

In India 150 years ago, in the area of Dornakal, there was a man called Venkaya who could neither read nor write. He heard from a friend about a new religion that was of a God that loved everyone. One day as he watched the Hindu pilgrims bathing in the river he was asked by one of their leaders why he was not bathing. He said he no longer believed enough in the Hindu ways. The leader asked if he was a Christian and Venkaya said, 'No, but I would like to be.' The leader told him of an English Christian preacher who could help him. Venkaya sought out Mr Darling who was a missionary with the Church Missionary Society. At that moment Mr Darling was deeply distressed: he had spoken of Christ for eight years and had not had one convert. Now, amid much opposition, Mr Darling taught and then baptised Venkaya and sixteen other outcasts. The seed was beginning to grow. In his old age and quite blind, Venkaya sat by the roadside to tell others the Gospel story. Through his preaching 500 converts were baptised. His work continues to bear fruit.

41 Weeding out the harmful

Aim

To show that although good and evil are woven into our lives, we must at some stage weed out the harmful.

Reading

Matthew 13:24-30, 36-43

Illustration

They were known as the terrible twins at school. They were disruptive in class and caused no end of bother in the playground. They were encouraging other children to be disruptive too. Staff meetings talked about them, offered ideas to help them, but all were determined to keep them in the class if possible. Teachers used their skill and discernment in dealing with them. It was only in the third year that it became obvious that it could not go on. By then it was also obvious it was not both of them but just one who was the real trouble. They were put in separate year groups. Now one settled down and worked hard. The other continued to be trouble at school and at home. The school finally had to remove the disruptive one from the normal class. They were reluctant to do so but it needed doing. Though they were twins with apparently equal opportunities, one caused trouble all his life; the other became a doctor and a healer.

42 The kingdom of heaven

Aim

To show how we need to search for the kingdom; we need to sow and sift out the good from the bad.

Reading

Matthew 13:(31-33), 44-52

Illustration

Every so often we hear of someone finding a great treasure. These days metal detectors are often used to go over fields and ancient sites to turn up all sorts of wonderful things. Sometimes it is the work of archaeologists who patiently, carefully and slowly remove piles of debris before they get to the treasure they are looking for.

In 1947 a Bedouin shepherd boy was looking for a sheep that had strayed. Spying a cave in the cliff face, he decided to come back with a friend and explore. In the cave they found large earthenware pots with scrolls inside wrapped in linen. They were treasure indeed, for they were the Dead Sea Scrolls and the place was Qumran. In time the scrolls were sold and the boy compensated. All the caves in the vicinity were searched and more scrolls were found. A sect of Jews around the time that Jesus lived had written the scrolls. Many insights into the world that Jesus lived in have come from the deciphering and reading of these scrolls – they are a treasure indeed.

43 Enough for all

Aim

To show that the compassion of Jesus can reach out to others through our willingness to give and share.

Reading

Matthew 14:13-21

Illustration

This is the story of the 'long spoons'. Someone was given a vision of what life is like. She went into a room where there was a lot of food to be eaten but only by a long spoon. The spoon was so long that the people could not get it to their mouths and food was being spilled and wasted. Everyone looked frustrated and hungry. It looked like a picture of hell.

Then she went into another room where there were still long spoons and the same system. Here everyone was feeding someone else. They were reaching out and feeding a neighbour. Here there was much laughter and fellowship. It felt more like heaven than hell.

She thought long on this and realised that there is enough in the world for everyone's need but not for their greed.

44 The storms of life

Aim

To show that our God cares and is with us in the storms of life.

Reading

Matthew 14:22-33

Illustration

At lifeboat stations there is usually a record of rescues and of the wonderful bravery of those who went out in the storms to help others. Sometimes, instead of a record of rescue, it simply says, 'Standing by'. That is when the lifeboat was there and ready to help if needed. The crew were keeping a watch and were ready to come to the aid of a troubled vessel if called to do so. How often our God is like that – 'standing by', always ready to help those who call upon him.

Julian of Norwich lived through stormy times. It was the time of the Black Death, the Peasants' Revolt, the battles of Crécy, Poitiers and Agincourt. She saw four kings sit on the throne of England. As a young woman, she had nearly died but she could write:

> He did not say, 'You shall not be tempest-tossed; you shall not be work-weary; you shall not be distressed.' But he did say, 'You shall not be overcome.'

Julian was deeply aware that God is 'our maker, our lover and our keeper'. Amidst the storms of life, Julian was aware of the presence, the love and the power of God.

We need to learn to put our hand into the hand of God who never leaves us or forsakes us.

45 God's love is not exclusive

Aim

To show that God's love is not exclusive but is offered to all people, in all places and at all times.

Reading

Matthew 15:(10-20), 21-28

Illustration

We may hate what a person does but we need to learn not to hate the person. It is said that God hates sin but loves the sinner. The more exclusive we become in our dealings, the smaller our world and our heart. God's love is not exclusive.

There is a story of a young man who tried to join a famous London club. He had tried for months and was refused entry for one reason or another. The club was determined to be exclusive. The man's background, place of schooling, position in society did not suit. He was a good man but firmly kept out. In his prayers he asked why this was so. Then, in a vision one night, Jesus came and spoke to him and said, 'I would not worry, you have tried for months to get in; I have tried for years and they have kept me out!' See Matthew 25:45. Consider Edwin Markham's words:

> He drew a circle that shut me out –
> Rebel, heretic, thing to flout.
> But love and I had the wit to win –
> We drew a circle and brought him in.

46 Not what, but whom

Aim

To show that Jesus is the Christ, our Saviour.

Reading

Matthew 16:13-20

Illustration

Many people ask 'What do you believe in?' but for Christians it is not *what* but *whom*. We believe in the living Christ. We believe that Jesus is the Son of God and is our Saviour. We seek a living relationship with him.

Not what but whom

Not what, but whom, I do believe
that in my darkest hour of need
hath comfort that no mortal creed
to mortal man may give;
not what but whom!
For Christ is more than all the creeds
and his full life of gentle deeds
shall all the creeds outlive.
Not what I do believe but whom!
Who walks beside me in the gloom?
Who shares the burden wearisome?
Who all the dim way doth illume,
and bids me look beyond the tomb
the larger life to live?
Not what I do believe but whom!
Not what, but whom!

John Oxenham

47 Seek first God's will

Aim

To show that we need to resist those, even loved ones, who prevent us from doing the will of God.

Reading

Matthew 16:21-28

Illustration

When the devil cannot get at us directly he will seek to lead us astray by our friends. It is sad how many people are led astray by friends and family. Sometimes our loved ones are only seeking to protect us but in so doing they stop us risking for God.

Columbanus was born in Ireland about 540 AD. He was of noble birth, strong and intelligent and destined to be a ruler of people. Columbanus heard the call of God and decided to dedicate his life to God in a monastery. His poor mother was heartbroken. He could have such a wonderful career and he was hardly ready to leave home. She tried to stop him, at first holding on to him and then lying down across the doorway sobbing. It was very difficult for Columbanus but he had set his sights on serving God. He stepped purposefully over his mother and set out for the monastery. If he had stayed at home, we would never have heard of him, but in time he became one of the greatest missionaries and teachers in Europe.

48 Forgiveness rebuilds relationships

Aim
To show that we should seek forgiveness and the rebuilding of relationships.

Reading
Matthew 18:15-20

Illustration
In the story *Great Expectations* by Charles Dickens, Pip has dealt badly with Joe the blacksmith who cared for him in his early days. When Pip was ill and in debt, Joe came to care for him. Joe stayed by him, gave him cooling drinks.

> At last, one day, I took courage, and said, 'Is it Joe?'
>
> And the dear old home-voice answered, 'Which it air, old chap.'
>
> 'Oh Joe, you break my heart! Look angry at me, Joe! Strike me, Joe! Tell me of my ingratitude. Don't be so good to me.'
>
> For Joe had actually laid his head down on the pillow at my side and put his arm around my neck, in his joy that I knew him.
>
> 'Which dear old Pip, old chap,' said Joe, 'you and me was ever friends. And when you are well enough to go out for a ride – what larks!'
>
> After which Joe withdrew to the window and stood with his back towards me, wiping his eyes. And as my extreme weakness prevented me going to him, I lay there penitently whispering, 'O God bless him! God bless this gentle Christian man!'

49 Forgiveness has no limits

Aim

To show there are no limits to God's love and forgiveness.

Reading

Matthew 18:21-35

Illustration

When John Wesley was sailing to America he witnessed the keel-hauling of a member of the crew for an offence on board ship. This was a particularly cruel form of punishment as it meant being tied to a rope, thrown overboard, drawn under the vessel and out the other side. There was always the chance you would drown or perish in some other way. The captain said to John Wesley as they watched, 'You see, Mr Wesley, I never forgive.' It was not for John Wesley to question the captain's power of command but he could and did question that statement. He replied, 'Then, sir, I hope that you never sin!'

50 God's generosity

Aim

To show how caring and generous God is.

Reading

Matthew 20:1-16

Illustration

Theo kept strange accounts. He gave equally and generously to all who worked for him. He did not count one worth more than another. All who were willing and able to work were given a whole day's pay whether they had been asked to work all day or only for an hour. It was the same with his relationships: he cared for all equally. Some thought that they clocked up a bigger balance for reward and expected to receive more. But Theo loved all equally. Some grumbled about this but in truth they were trying to buy his love and affection when it was freely given to all. There are always people who grumble.

The only people Theo could not help were those who chose to turn away from him. Even these he gladly would give to if they allowed him to. Theo kept strange accounts.

51 Words and deeds

Aim

To look at making choices and practising what we profess.

Reading

Matthew 21:23-32

Illustration

In a community there was a group of people who were always ready to say, 'Yes, sir. Three bags full, sir.' They appeared to be willing to take on anything that was asked and always talked with respect. They appeared only too willing, ready and able. But when it came to the crunch they were too busy, too tired, couldn't be bothered, or had just forgotten what they had promised. When they were needed they did not turn up.

There was another group who always seemed reluctant. They did not particularly want to get involved. They had other things to do. Yet when they were aware of the need they had a change of heart and waded in. They would not profess to be part of any system, but out of love and care they got on board and did what was needed.

It was hard to depend on either group but in the end the second group was more likely to get things done.

52 Care for God's world

Aim

To appreciate all that God has given us and act responsibly.

Reading

Matthew 21:33-46

Illustration

The group was given a new hall through the generosity of others and through national grants. But from the start they did not appreciate it. The walls were daubed with graffiti, the floor was covered with litter; inside the building they ran riot. Though people tried to care for them, they rejected any offers of oversight or help. In time the hall looked derelict and no one dared to go and look after it. Windows were broken and toilets were vandalised.

Sadly after all the efforts of some the hall was shut down. Those who were given it were causing too much trouble. It became a liability. The idea had been a good one but the group did not appreciate this. Finally it was dismantled and the land given to others.

53 RSVP

Aim

To show that we are invited to share the joys of the kingdom in the presence of the King, but that it is up to us to accept that invitation.

Reading

Matthew 22:1-14

Illustration

Richard and Judy were invited to the palace to meet the king to enjoy sharing in the beauty of the surroundings and to take part in a banquet. It was a most generous invitation and they wondered what they had done to deserve it. In fact, it was sent out because of the love of the king. They showed lots of people the invitation with pride. They put it where it could be seen in their house. Most days they looked at it and said how wonderful it was. They had advance warning of the date and slowly it came near. One day Judy looked at her calendar and said, 'Oh, I am supposed to get my hair done today – what shall I do?'

Richard replied, 'That's OK. Just go ahead. I fancy doing some gardening.' For all their talk and show, they counted the invitation of little value. By excusing themselves, they excluded themselves.

54 Give God his due

Aim

To show that we must give God his due.

Reading

Matthew 22:15-22

Illustration

One of the greatest witnesses to giving God his due was the early Christian martyrs. Catherine, who gives her name to the 'Catherine Wheel' firework, was born of a noble family and lived in the fourth century. The emperor was attracted to her and wanted to marry her. Catherine refused because she was already a 'bride of Christ'. She is said to have disputed with 50 philosophers whose job it was to convince her of her error and she defeated them. Because she refused to do as commanded by the emperor she was tortured by being fastened to a large wheel and driven around the arena – but the wheel broke. Finally she was beheaded.

55 Love your neighbour

Aim

To encourage us to love God with our whole being.

Reading

Matthew 22:34-46

Illustration

'Christmas wouldn't be Christmas without any presents,' Jo had grumbled as she waited with her three sisters until their mother returned from church . . .

> 'Merry Christmas, Marmee! Many of them!'
>
> 'Merry Christmas, little daughters! But I want to say one word before we sit down. Not far away from here lies a poor woman with a little newborn baby. Six children are huddled into one bed to keep from freezing, for they have no fire. There is nothing to eat over there, and the oldest boy came to tell me they are suffering from hunger and cold. My girls, will you give them your breakfast as a Christmas present?'
>
> They were all unusually hungry having waited nearly an hour, and for a minute no one spoke – only a minute, for Jo exclaimed impetuously, 'I am so glad you came before we began!'
>
> 'May I go and help to carry the things to the poor children?' asked Beth eagerly.
>
> 'I shall take the cream and the muffins,' added Amy, heroically giving up the articles she most liked.
>
> Meg was already covering the buckwheats, and piling the bread into one big plate.
>
> 'I thought you would do it,' said Mrs March, smiling as if satisfied. 'You shall have bread and milk for breakfast and make up for it at dinner time.'
>
> They were soon ready, and the procession set out.
>
> Fortunately it was early and they went through the back streets, so few people saw them, and no one laughed at the queer party.

A poor bare miserable room it was with broken windows, no fire, ragged bedclothes, a sick mother, wailing baby and a group of pale, hungry children huddled under one old quilt to keep warm.

How the big eyes stared and the blue lips smiled as the girls went in!

'Ach mein Gott. It is good angels come to us!' said the poor woman crying for joy.

Little Women, Louisa May Alcott (1868)

56 The Beatitudes

Aim

To show that blessedness comes from God.

Reading

Matthew 5:1-12

Illustration

The word 'blessed' comes from the Greek word 'makarios' and is used to describe the gods. Jesus uses it to describe those who do God's will. The Greeks called Cyprus the 'blessed island' or the 'happy island' because it was such a rich and fertile land with a good climate, rich in minerals and natural resources. Fruit and grain and flowers could grow in abundance. It was a place where people should be perfectly happy. It should be a place of peace and harmony. In the same way, those who lived the beatitudes would find peace and harmony in God's presence and God's love.

57 Good News in dark times

Aim

To show that our God cares for us in all our troubles and that his kingdom is near.

Reading

Matthew 24:1-14

Illustration

When we have dark or bad days we need to remind ourselves that God is with us and cares for us. Here is a prayer from the Hebrides which you may find helpful:

> Though the dawn breaks cheerless on this Isle today,
> my spirit walks in a path of light.
> For I know my greatness.
> Thou has built me a throne within thy heart.
> I dwell safely within the circle of thy care.
> I cannot for a moment fall out of the everlasting arms.
> I am on my way to thy glory.
>
> *Hebridean Altars,* Alistair Maclean (1937)

Now that is Good News, whatever the day!

58 Due care and attention

Aim

To show how we need to keep ourselves aware that Jesus comes to us.

Reading

Matthew 25:1-13

Illustration

John could have learnt much more at school but he was always fooling around or thinking about what he was going to do after school. He never listened. He was there in body but not in mind or spirit.

Jean knew it was no use talking to her father while he was watching a football match on the television. He was in the same room but he was not really where she was and he would not hear.

There is a danger that we are never really aware of our Lord's coming and we miss the wonderful relationship that is offered to us: we miss the moment even though it is offered to us more than once. Too often Jesus finds we are 'not there' when he comes. He seeks us out but we do not give him any attention. Think of Jesus saying:

> I called your name but you were out or preoccupied.
>
> I came to you in the night but you did not notice.
>
> I knocked on your door and your heart but they remained closed.
>
> I asked for your help but you were too busy.
>
> I wanted to know you, to give my love to you, but you were otherwise engaged.

59 Use it or lose it

Aim

To encourage the awareness that we all have talents to share and develop, and that we must use them.

Reading

Matthew 25:14-30

Illustration

Millie was now quite old but she always had a strange attitude to gifts. If she was given a present, she would thank the person profusely and say how kind it was of them to give her a gift. She said she would treasure it. Then without unwrapping it she put it away in a drawer for another day. When a niece came to help her to move she discovered many unused gifts, still wrapped. There were biscuits and cakes that had moulded away; there were jars of things that had long passed their sell-by date; there were clothes that now would no longer fit Millie. Drawer after drawer of gifts were put out in the bin. Because she did not use them she lost them; she never had the benefit of them.

In the same way we will lose our local small shops unless we use them. We will lose bus services unless we use them. We will lose our God-given gifts and talents unless we use them. The thing we need understand is 'Use it or lose it'.

60 As you did to the least of these

Aim

To make people aware that Christ comes to us in our encounter with others and in the needs of the poor.

Reading

Matthew 25:31-46

Illustration

Christopher wanted to serve the king. He wanted to go to the palace and give himself to serve the king. But he was held up. First he had to look after aging parents. When he set off he had a gift for the king but he met a poor family who had been robbed of their belongings and he gave the gift to them. Later on he met a family whose cart had stuck deep in the mud. He stayed to help them and got sprayed with mud. Now he had no gift and his fine clothes were filthy. He felt he could not journey on but something encouraged him – words he had heard long ago. When he finally reached the palace, he received a royal welcome. He was about to apologise for the state he was in but the king said, 'You have been a great help to me over the years, in the way you cared for your parents, in the way you gave to the poor and when you helped those in need. I was there and it was me you gave your help and love to. Welcome to the fullness of the kingdom which you have served for a long time.'

Topical index

Numbers refer to illustrations and not to pagination.

Bible reference index

Numbers refer to illustrations and not to pagination.